FROM CONDEMNATION TO CHRIST: THE ROAD TO EVANGELISM

Matt Hertzberg

Published by Matt Hertzberg, 2024.

FROM CONDEMNATION TO CHRIST:
THE ROAD TO EVANGELISM

Copyright © 2024 by Matthew R. Hertzberg

First Edition 2024

Scripture quotations are taken from the Holy Bible, The King James Version (KJV) 1987 and The American Standard Version (ASV) 1901.

© All rights reserved. No part of this book may be reproduced in any form without written permission from the publisher.

Table of Contents

INTRODUCTION 1
CHAPTER 1 5
CHAPTER 2 9
CHAPTER 3 13
CHAPTER 4 21
CHAPTER 5 25
CHAPTER 6 27
CHAPTER 7 31
CHAPTER 8 37
CHAPTER 9 41
CHAPTER 10 45
CHAPTER 11 49
CHAPTER 12 53
CHAPTER 13 57

THIS BOOK IS DEDICATED TO GOD, TO MY WIFE, AND TO MY FAMILY AND FRIENDS

Without God nothing would be possible, because God created everything. Because of God we breathe. Because of God we have reason and logic. Because of God we get to live on this beautiful planet. It is he who came down in human flesh and died on the cross for the forgiveness of our sins by washing them away with his own blood and was resurrected three days later so we all could be saved and have everlasting life in heaven with him. Everyday God gives me the wisdom, power, courage, and strength to keep learning and growing in my faith and his guiding hands keep pushing me, never letting me waver in the command that he gave to all of us Christians which is to preach the gospel to all creation. Like Jesus said in Matthew 19:26, "With God all things are possible." To my beautiful and loving wife for being so supportive and understanding through all of these years. I love you honey, always and forever! To my family and friends for the love and support they have given me. I have been tremendously blessed with the abundance of love that has surrounded me my entire life. Words can't express the gratitude that I have for everyone of you. Thank you! I love you all!

"JESUS CHRIST DIED ON THE CROSS FOR THE FORGIVENESS OF OUR SINS, AND WAS RESURRECTED THREE DAYS LATER SO WE COULD BE SAVED AND HAVE ETERNAL LIFE IN HEAVEN WITH HIM."

INTRODUCTION

It's early Saturday morning. The world around me is finally waking up. Cars are slowly filling the streets. I pull up to my first destination. As I get out of my vehicle with a GoPro securely around my neck. Gripping my gospel tracts and a sign that reads, "REPENT AND BELIEVE THE GOSPEL! STOP SINNING! FOLLOW JESUS!" As I get into position, I open up my mouth, and in the blink of an eye, the Holy Spirit starts flowing out of me with fierce compassion, courage, and love. Let me ask you something, is this the way your weekend always begins too, or is it just me? Hello friends. My name is Matt. I'm an Evangelist and a Christian Apologist. I'm also the founder of "Spreading the Seed of Truth." It's a YouTube channel dedicated to spreading the word of God to all creation while immersing them in the name of the Father, and the Son, and the Holy Spirit. In this book I'm going to talk about Christianity and compare it to other belief systems throughout the world and aim to destroy the walls of fear and the stigma that surrounds evangelism hoping to encourage other Christians to take their first steps towards evangelism. I'm going to explain the three methods of evangelism. Private One on One, Public One on One, and finally spreading the gospel of Jesus Christ by Open-air

Preaching. I'm also going to talk about the situations that you might encounter while evangelizing, and about the do's and don'ts of all the things you'll need to know as you continue down the road of evangelism learning and growing in your faith, in wisdom, in courage, and in truth.

LET'S PRAY

Our Father who art in heaven,

We pray that you give us the wisdom and strength to conquer any fear towards evangelism that we may have, and to keep learning and growing in our faith, and to give us the courage we need to go forth and spread the good news of your Son. We pray that through your words we see the way, the truth, and the life in your Son's name Jesus Christ we pray, Amen.

CHAPTER 1

OUR PURPOSE IN LIFE

Evangelism. It's a scary word. There are three methods of evangelism and less than 10% of Christians actually do them on a consistent basis. What is evangelism? It's the spreading of the Christian gospel of Jesus Christ by public speaking or personal witness. The Greek word for gospel is "evangelion" which means "good news." The good news is Jesus Christ, Son of God, God himself, our Creator, was resurrected three days later after dying on the cross, sacrificing himself for the forgiveness of our sins so we all can be saved and have everlasting life in heaven with him. It's been over fifteen years now since I gave my life over to Jesus Christ and have been learning and growing in my faith ever since. My journey with evangelism started quickly. There was no dipping my toes in the water here. It was a full on cannonball right into the deep end. As soon as the Holy Spirit called I answered. Not only do I evangelize on the streets, but I also go to the churches of the Mormons, the Jehovah's Witnesses, the Catholics and to the Islamic Centers to explain to them the contradictions between what they believe in and what the word of God actually says. In order for me to do this, I had to study their beliefs and do my own research. I'm sure you can imagine how interesting these conversations can be. The road to evangelism is different for every Christian, but every Christian has the ability to do all three of these evangelism methods. It's all about how far are you willing to push yourself out of your comfort zone and how far are you willing to go to glorify God. Without evangelism. Without spreading the word of God. Without spreading the good news of Jesus Christ, how are people going to know about it if they haven't read the bible. If they've turned their backs on God, or if they've been deceived or lied to. We are all God's creation, and he loves us all. He wants us to know him and have fellowship with him. Evangelism is the only way we can get this information of truth out to them. This is why evangelism is so important. If they're not going to search for it themselves, or if they have no idea on where to find it, that's why we have to go to them. I understand that evangelism can be done through the many platforms that we have available now with YouTube, Facebook, TikTok, ect..., but I'm just going to focus on the original form of evangelism. How it all began. Face to face, personal, out in the world preaching the word of God. Glorifying him with all of our heart, soul, and mind one on one. Although evangelism through these technological platforms is a great way and the easiest way to get God's word out to all creation, I think all Christians should take advantage of this wonderful technology and use it to spread the gospel to the world. Personally though, in my experience, evangelizing to people on the streets, physically face to face, not through a video or comment replies on your phone or computer, has a next level human element to it that's not found on YouTube or any of the other platforms. We get to read each other's voices, each other's gestures. The situation is tangible. It's physical and verbally real. The aspect of teaching and the depths of it is tremendous. By describing answers and questions in great detail using all the tools we have. I just feel the connection on the streets evangelizing in a personal face to face situation can bring out a part of humanity that is lost through a video or a text. Plus, they won't ever admit this, but when anyone sees an evangelist, part of them actually respects their zeal. Going out and taking on the hatred, and the world's disagreement and standing up for what they believe in. Doing it all for the glory of God. Our purpose in life is not to win the Super Bowl or to make a million dollars. Our purpose in life is to glorify God and to have fellowship with him. 1st Corinthians 10:31, "Whether therefore ye eat, or drink, or whatsoever ye do, do all to the glory of God."

"OUR PURPOSE IN LIFE IS TO GLORIFY GOD AND TO HAVE FELLOWSHIP WITH HIM."

CHAPTER 2

THE BIBLE: ALL SCRIPTURE IS GOD-BREATHED

We as humans are all searching for truth, but there's only one place you can find it. The Holy Bible. John 17:17, "Sanctify them through thy truth: thy word is truth." What it's saying here is that "GOD'S WORD IS TRUTH!" The BIBLE is TRUTH! 2nd Timothy 3:16, "All scripture is given by inspiration of God, and is profitable for doctrine, for reproof, for correction, for instruction in righteousness." Without a doubt the bible is one of the greatest miracles of all time. Spanning two thousand years, three continents, in three different languages, sixty-six different books, forty different authors from all walks of life. Hundreds of years between books, and in some cases a thousand years, and there is not one contradiction, not one error. This could never be possible without divine inspiration. God used these selected people as his personal pencil to write these sixty-six love letters to us. The bible explains who God is, his love for us, his nature, how to have fellowship with him, our purpose in life, prophecies made and fulfilled throughout the bible with detailed pinpoint accuracy about future events and the coming Messiah, Our Savior, Jesus Christ. When we read the bible my friends, we have to let God's word speak to us. When we open a magazine or some other book to read it, do we think to ourselves, "How am I going to interpret this?" Of course not. We let the words speak to us. That's exactly how we should read the bible. We need to not worry about how we're going to interpret the bible. We just need to let the bible speak to us, not let us speak for the bible. That's why there's so many other beliefs out there. People have taken the word of God and made their own interpretation of how they want the bible to fit in with their own ideas, to fit in with their own pride and greed, to fit in with their own subjective well-being. We need to read the whole bible, and when we compare verses with others throughout the sixty-six books, you will see the unbelievable consistency of information that makes it whole. Now if you want to dive deeper into God's word because of questions that you may have or just because you want to learn more, that's awesome! Go right ahead! We all should be doing that. It really gives you a greater appreciation and understanding for the beautiful word of God. The answers to your questions are there and God's words will never vanish. Remember what Jesus Christ said in Matthew 24:35, "Heaven and earth shall pass away, but my words shall not pass away."

"SANCTIFY THEM THROUGH THY TRUTH: THY WORD IS TRUTH."
JOHN 17:17

CHAPTER 3

CHRISTIANITY: BELIEVING IN THE TRUTH

Let me tell you about Christianity my friends. Being part of Christianity is being a follower of Jesus Christ, a follower of The Holy Bible, a follower of God's word. That is what a Christian is. Before any Christian speaks or acts, the first few questions that should enter their mind is, "What would Jesus do?" "What would Jesus say?" "How would Jesus act?" We are to deny ourselves. Jesus said in Luke 9:23, "If any man will come after me, let him deny himself, and take up his cross daily, and follow me." Jesus also said in 1st John 2:6, "He that saith he abideth in him ought himself also so to walk, even as he walked." We are to walk in the footsteps of Jesus Christ. We are to live our life as he lived his. listen carefully my friends. What I'm about to say might blow your mind. Are you ready? Christianity is not a religion. Yes, you read that correctly. Christianity is not a religion. It's all about our relationship with God. To have fellowship with him, to love him, to care for him, to embrace him, just as he does for us. That's not a religion my friends, that's a relationship. Judaism (The Old Testament) and Christianity (The New

Testament) are book ends to the bible and are created by God, the only two belief systems in the world created by God, but the reason why Judaism is considered a religion and Christianity is not is because Judaism was about obedience to the law not for salvation, but to show that they were God's people and to receive blessings and protection from God, while Christianity is about God becoming the source of salvation. It's through Jesus Christ the Son of God that we are saved, blessed, and protected not by obedience, but by God's grace through our faith in the life, death, and resurrection of Jesus Christ. His sacrifice on the cross. The washing away of our sins and giving us everlasting life in heaven. It doesn't matter what we do. Our works will not save us. Jesus Christ did all the work for us. All God wants from us is to have fellowship with him. He wants us to love and enjoy him completely just as he loves and enjoys us. Unfortunately Judaism morphed into a contradiction of itself. Turning their back on God and his word. They deny the whole New Testament and the clear prophecies of Jesus Christ as the coming Messiah, the Son of God, God himself as mentioned in The Old Testament. They deny Jesus being the Creator of all things. They deny his nature and deity. They deny his resurrection and the sacrifice that he made for the whole world so we all could be saved. They believe that the old covenant is still in effect because they deny the New Testament which means they deny the new covenant, and for them, they're still waiting for the prophesied Messiah to come. Fortunately there are Jews in the world who do believe in the whole word of God. The whole bible. The Old and New Testaments, and that they believe the old covenant has ended with Christ and he himself has given us the new covenant, and believing in everything that Our Lord and Savior Jesus Christ has done for us. Evidence is key for something to be considered true. I don't know about you, but I want evidence for something before I believe in it. I don't go by blind faith when it comes to belief systems. It's like if I were to say to you that God was throwing down bacon cheeseburgers from the sky, which I have to admit would be pretty awesome, you wouldn't just take my word for it and take it as truth. You would want to see the evidence for yourself, and if I didn't have any evidence to back up my claim, it would just be an empty claim, false, not true. Every claim we make is an empty claim until we present evidence to prove that it's true. Judaism and Christianity are The Old and New Testaments combined to complete the bible. To complete the whole word of God. The old covenant of The Old Testament ended after the death, burial, and resurrection of Christ, Romans 10:4, "For Christ is the end of the law for righteousness to every one that believeth." The new covenant began after the death of Jesus Christ, Matthew 26:27-28, "And he took the cup, and gave thanks, and gave it to them, saying," "Drink ye all of it; For this is my blood of the new testament, (new covenant) which is shed for many for the remission of sins." Mormons, Jehovah's Witnesses, and Catholicism use The Old and New Testament as their backdrop. As for Islam, they use parts of The Old and New Testament, but yet they believe that it's been corrupted and that they deny the deity of Jesus Christ, of him being the Son of God, God in human flesh and our Creator. They deny that Jesus Christ died on the cross for our sins and that he was resurrected three days later to save us all. Catholicism is guilty of practicing idolatry. They pray to and bow down to statues of Mary and the saints. They treat them as mediators, and that contradicts 1st Timothy 2:5, "For there is one God, and one mediator between God and men, the man Christ Jesus," and it contradicts Exodus 20:4-6, the second commandment. When Christ died on the cross, the veil in the temple was torn in two symbolizing the sacrifice that Christ made with the shedding of his own blood which was for the forgiveness of our sins. In that moment the way into the Holy of Holies was open to everyone through Jesus Christ, and it marked the start of the new covenant and the end of the old covenant. Catholicism also believes in purgatory which means that they believe the sacrifice Jesus Christ made on the cross for us wasn't enough. They believe that we still have to be purified in death before we go to heaven. That's what purgatory is, while 1st John 1:9 says, "If we confess our sins, he is faithful and just to forgive us our sins, and to cleanse (purify) us from all unrighteousness." Jesus Christ died on the cross for our purification of sins. Why do we have to be purified again in death when we have already been purified in life through Jesus Christ? That's a contradiction to 1st John 1:9 my friends. Mormons, and Jehovah's Witnesses deny Jesus as being the one and only God and Creator of all things which contradicts John 1:1-3, "In the beginning was the Word, and the Word was with God, and the Word was God. The same was in the beginning with God. All things were made by him; and without him was not any thing made that was made." Then in John 1:14 it says, "And the Word was made flesh, and dwelt among us." THE WORD IS JESUS CHRIST MY FRIENDS, which means that JESUS IS GOD and the CREATOR OF ALL THINGS! Hebrews 1:1-2 and Colossians 1:16 also talks about Jesus Christ being the Creator of all things. Jesus himself also claims many times in the bible to be God. He makes this claim in John 8:58, John 10:30, John 14:9, Revelation 22:13, and many others, and the evidence of the resurrection of Jesus Christ after three days proves to us that he is who he said he was, God in human flesh, Our Lord and Savior. The truth is all through the bible my friends. To make matters worse, all of these beliefs subscribe to a works for salvation system. All of these things contradict the word of God. Mind you, this list is just a small sample of the many contradictions they are guilty of. The founders Joseph Smith of the Mormons, Charles Taze Russell of the Jehovah's Witnesses, Muhammad of Islam, and the Catholic and Roman Catholic churches which follow the early church traditions that are filled with the pride and greed of men (which by the way, all of these founders had come hundreds of years after Jesus Christ) have all twisted scripture to fit their own beliefs, in some cases totally denied books of the bible and claimed them as corrupt, and changed God's original word to make their own gospel to preach to the world, a false gospel, a gospel not of the bible, Galatians 1:9 says, "As we said before, so say I now again, if any man preach any other gospel unto you than that ye have received, let him be accursed," and by doing that, they've falsified, changed, and contradicted God's word, Deuteronomy 4:2, "Ye shall not add unto the word which I command you, neither shall ye diminish ought from it, that ye may keep the commandments of the Lord your God which I command you." The thing is, they don't have the evidence to back up their reasoning on why they've contradicted the word of God, and why there's no evidence to prove the existence of some of the people, places, and things found in some of these books that they claim are the word of God like The Book of Mormon, The New World Translation, and The Qur'an. Catholics are a little different in that not all of them believe in the contradictions that go against the bible. Some Catholics actually stay true to God's original word. As for all the other beliefs out there surrounding Paganism, Monotheism, Cultism, philosophy, reincarnation, ect..., they were all created by man, and are all work for salvation based, and they all contradict the word of God. Christianity is the only belief system that knows where they're going when they die. Philippians 3:20, "For our citizenship is in heaven; whence also we wait for a Saviour, the Lord Jesus Christ." Ephesians 1:13-14 says, "In whom he also trusted, after that ye heard the word of truth, the gospel of your salvation: in whom also after that ye believed, ye were sealed with that Holy Spirit of promise, Which is the earnest of our inheritance until the redemption of the purchased possession, unto the praise of his glory." If you believe and trust in Jesus Christ and the gospels of him that reside in the bible, you are going to heaven. No work on your part needs to be done. Remember, Jesus Christ did all the work for us. As for everyone else, they believe works or works plus grace will save them. Unfortunately for them, the question is, how much work is enough work to get to heaven, or their version of heaven? Besides Christianity, no one knows where they're going when they die. That's the truth my friends. The evidence in the bible proves this. Remember, evidence is key.

Atheism also falls into the same situation where the lack of evidence is undeniable. No evidence equals empty claims filled with delusions and lies. We need to pray for all of these lost poor souls who have been lied to and have suppressed the truth for so many years. The Old and New Testaments of the bible on the other hand has evidence to prove its claims. The evidence surrounds us all. For God we have the perfect precision of order, creation, and design of this universe, of this world, of us. This planet of ours, the only planet that can sustain human life. Our reasoning, our logic, our conscience, our morality. All of this wasn't by accident my friends. All the eyewitness testimonies recorded in the bible and all the recorded writings that were created outside of the bible on the life, death, burial, and resurrection of Jesus Christ. The divine inspiration of the bible is filled with fulfilled prophecies. The Dead Sea Scrolls, and then there's the archaeological evidence of the bible that proves its historical accuracy. The evidence is there. Just do the research and you'll know the truth. Don't take my word for it my friends, take God's word.

"IN THE BEGINNING WAS THE WORD, AND THE WORD WAS WITH GOD, AND THE WORD WAS GOD. THE SAME WAS IN THE BEGINNING WITH GOD. ALL THINGS WERE MADE BY HIM; AND WITHOUT HIM WAS NOT ANY THING MADE THAT WAS MADE."
JOHN 1:1-3

CHAPTER 4

GOD'S LOVE AND GRACE

If we deny God's word, we deny God himself, and by doing that we deny truth. God loves us all and wants us to be in heaven with him. It's through the grace of God that we are saved. Ephesians 2:8-9, "For by grace are ye saved through faith; and that not of yourselves: it is the gift of God: Not of works, lest any man should boast." Grace means "undeserved favor." It cannot be earned. It is freely given to us by God. Anyone who believes that works by their own doing will either save them or will help save them is contradicting the bible. THEY'RE CONTRADICTING THE WORD OF GOD! God would never contradict himself, so why would we ever contradict God. We are all born sinners my friends. Psalm 51:5, "Behold, I was shapen iniquity; and in sin did my mother conceive me." Romans 3:23, "For all have sinned, and come short of the glory of God." Romans 3:10, "As it is written, There is none righteous, no, not one." We all deserve eternal punishment and death because we all have sinned against God, Romans 6:23, "For the wages of sin is death." It would be just like your father on earth disciplining you for disobeying him. It's no different, except with God being eternal, the consequence is also eternal. I know that might sound scary, but God is fair and a just judge over all of his creation. He will not punish those who don't deserve it. He will judge us accordingly by the choices that we make. It's all up to us. We choose if we want to be separated from God or not. We choose if we are going to heaven or hell by either choosing God or not choosing God. The choice is all ours. We need to understand that. It's not God's fault if we go to hell, it's ours. God loves us so much that he gave us a free will. A choice to love him or hate him. To turn to him or away from him. God wants us to love him unconditionally as he loves us unconditionally. God doesn't want any of us to suffer wrath. In 1st Thessalonians 5:9 it says, "For God hath not appointed us to wrath, but to obtain salvation by our Lord Jesus Christ." True love is never forced. True love is never bargained with. True love is never bought. True love is always freely given. That's what God wants from us, TRUE LOVE! That's why he didn't create robots. A lot of people ask, "If God is so good, why did he create evil?" Evil doesn't come from God. It comes from our abuse of our free will. Even though the moral law has been written in all of our hearts by God, Romans 2:15, we as humans choose to separate ourselves from God. We as humans want to follow our own path, our own desires. Even through all this, God loves us so much that he came down in human flesh and sacrificed himself through death to wash away our sins and rose three days later so we all could be saved and have eternal life in heaven with him. That's the greatest form of love. To sacrifice oneself for another, John 15:13, "Greater love hath no man than this, that a man lay down his life for his friends." Jesus Christ did that for us.

A sinless, prideless, perfect man like Jesus Christ, God in human flesh, putting all of our pain, suffering and sins on his shoulders. That's the good news! God gave us a way out through Jesus Christ. John 3:16, "For God so loved the world that he gave his only begotten Son, that whosoever believeth in him should not perish, but have everlasting life." John 14:6, "Jesus saith unto him, I am the way, the truth, and the life: no man cometh unto the Father, but by me." Jesus said in John 3:3, "Jesus answered and said unto him, Verily, verily, I say unto thee, Except a man be born again, he cannot see the kingdom of God." Once you trust and believe and confess with your mouth that Jesus is Lord, and believe the gospels and that God raised him from the dead, you will be saved and be born again. We are not children of God until we are born again. Once we are born again, a supernatural event happens when the Holy Spirit comes into us and we are given a new heart and a new spirit, Ezekiel 36:26. 2nd Corinthians 5:17, "Therefore if any man be in Christ, he is a new creature: old things are passed away; behold, all things are become new." When this happens, the Holy Spirit will teach us and guide us to the truth and in all things in remembrance of Jesus Christ. The things you once loved and followed from your human desires, actions, and words through your old heart, are things you no longer want in your life, because your old heart is gone and because you have now given your life to God. It's a supernatural situation given to us only by God.

"JESUS SAITH UNTO HIM, I AM THE WAY, THE TRUTH, AND THE LIFE: NO MAN COMETH UNTO THE FATHER, BUT BY ME." JOHN 14:6

CHAPTER 5

THE TRINITY OF CHRISTIANITY

The Trinity my friends. It's a mystery to many. The Trinity consists of God the Father, God the Son, and God the Holy Spirit. God is one being that exists as three divine persons. We are born in the image of God and according to his likeness. Because of that, like God the Father, we have a Trinity in ourselves, well, a human trinity if you will. Let me explain. We have a soul, flesh, and a spirit. The soul is our nature. Who we are as humans. The flesh is what we see everyday in the mirror. The spirit is how we connect with God. How we communicate with him. Now the Trinity of our eternal Father, it's God the Father as the soul, God the Son as the flesh, and God the Holy Spirit as the spirit. That's why Jesus could pray to God the Father while he was on earth. He prayed from the flesh, in the Holy Spirit, just like how we can pray to God the Father from our flesh in the Holy Spirit. Once you are in Jesus Christ, you will be free from eternal punishment. Romans 8:1, "There is therefore now no condemnation to them which are in Christ Jesus." Thus your life in Christ, your life as a Christian now begins.

"GOD IS ONE BEING THAT EXISTS AS THREE DIVINE PERSONS."

CHAPTER 6

THE GREAT COMMISSION

You have given your life to God. You're a follower of Jesus Christ. A dedicated Christian through and through. A follower of his commands, but one. The last one Jesus Christ had given not only to his apostles before his ascension, but to all of us as his disciples. It's called The Great Commission. He commanded us to evangelize. Matthew 28:19, "Go ye therefore, and make disciples of all the nations, baptizing them into the name of the Father and of the Son and of the Holy Spirit." Mark 16:15, "And he said unto them, Go ye into all the world, and preach the gospel to every creature." This world is full of sin my friends. Unfortunately this world will never find peace until it finds Jesus Christ. That's why it's so important to get God's word out to as many people as we can. We are God's instruments. He uses us to spread his word. To spread the gospel. We are spreading the seeds of truth, hoping for them to latch on to someone whose spirit is open, then God will do the rest. A seed can't grow with bad soil. It's the same thing with a person. If their spirit line is closed off, that's the same thing as having bad soil. That person needs an open spirit since the spirit is our communication line to God.

If that spirit line is closed off, God can't water those seeds to make them grow, and if God can't do that, that person won't see the truth, and won't know God. Christians feel safe in their church bubble contributing, and glorifying God, but what about the lost souls right outside those church walls. We can't forget about them. They too need the word of God. That's why evangelism is so important. Tomorrow is never guaranteed, my friends. This might be their last day to have a chance at salvation. We also as Christians must remember, evangelizing is for God's glory, not ours. Unfortunately for some of the evangelists that are on YouTube, Facebook, TikTok, or any of the other platforms, I'm worried about some of their true intentions. Are they doing it for God's glory, or has a little bit of pride and greed slipped in, and the views, sponsorships, money, and fame taken some of that glory away from God. Everything is for God's glory my friends. Let's not forget that. I want all Christians to ask themselves, "How am I going to glorify God today?" "Am I doing all that I can to glorify God?" "Am I doing all of this for my glory or for God's? Many Christians know the commands of The Great Commission, but don't think much about it. People are quick to talk about how they follow the Ten Commandments, but the command for evangelizing is just forgotten, ignored, or not thought of as important. Whatever the reason, it's the last command given to us by Jesus to ensure everyone has a chance to know God, to love God, and to have fellowship with God, all through Jesus Christ, so they can receive their inheritance in heaven.

"AND HE SAID UNTO THEM, GO YE INTO ALL THE WORLD, AND PREACH THE GOSPEL TO EVERY CREATURE."
MARK 16:15

CHAPTER 7

THE DO'S AND DON'TS AND THE STIGMA OF EVANGELISM

When you bring up evangelism to anyone, many people automatically think of a person holding a sign that says, "YOU'RE GOING TO BURN IN HELL." Yelling at people with some kind of sound system like a mic or a bullhorn saying that they're going to hell if they don't believe in Jesus Christ. The thing is, the image presented here isn't too far off, but the presentation of the message is where the stigma lies. Unfortunately I do see this kind of anger and attack played out from time to time. It's a situation that automatically shuts down any possibility of a conversation. It's something we as evangelists do not condone. I believe these people mean well, but haven't realized or for the moment lost the idea of Proverbs 15:1-2, "A soft answer turneth away wrath: but grievous words stir up anger. The tongue of the wise useth knowledge aright: but the mouth of fools poureth out foolishness." Unfortunately they're letting their emotions get the best of them, and are speaking directly from that aspect instead of their heart and spirit. Don't let your emotions consume you. A calm voice goes a long way.

When evangelizing by preaching, always preach and teach together. As an evangelist, we are here to get the gospel out to the world, but we are also here to teach. It's not about just preaching God's word, we need to explain God's word so people can understand it. We need to explain the evidence, the message, the world and the people within the bible. It doesn't do any good to preach the word of God without any substance behind it. When projecting your voice, using any kind of sound system is good for loud or big crowds or with loud music being played. Your voice needs to reach as many people as possible. If you're in an area where it's not too loud and no large crowds, just your regular voice will do just fine. It's more personable, and some people might not be so quickly turned off and shutdown. Remember, the key is to keep them listening, not to turn them away. Bringing them into the conversation is a must. Always speak with compassion, love, and an open heart. Yelling at people will only turn them away. You can start out by just giving your testimony, or asking them questions like, "Do you believe in Jesus?" "What do you believe in?" "Do you have any questions for me?" This kind of communication can open them up, and they're more willing to join in on the conversation instead of feeling like they're on the outside or being attacked. That's what every evangelist should strive to accomplish, engaging in conversation. We're spreading God's word, hoping it takes to someone with an open spirit to God and the truth. Hoping they hear God's voice before it's too late. You might run into people filled with anger, deceived by lies and delusions with different opinions and beliefs from all walks of life. The key here is to never forget why you are here. To spread the gospel of Jesus Christ to all creation. To spread the truth. Unfortunately many have suppressed the truth, Romans 1:18, "For the wrath of God is revealed from heaven against all ungodliness and unrighteousness of men, who hold the truth in unrighteousness." They don't realize that we're trying to save them from spiritual death. GoPros are essential for your protection. Just in case. It's rare, but it's better to have one and not need it then to need one and not have it. When spreading the gospel, signs and gospel tracts are a good tool to have as long as they're biblical. They're quite inexpensive, and you can find them easily online. Gospel tracts have the word of God on them and are used to spread the gospel of Jesus Christ. They're nice because you're actually giving them the word of God, and it's theirs to keep. They can't hide from the word of God when it's in their actual hands. Gospel signs help out in many ways. They can be great conversation starters. If you're engaged in a conversation with someone, that sign is there to keep spreading the gospel to all that see it, even when you're occupied with someone else. Sometimes people can't hear you. It might be too loud where they are or they're in a car driving by, but with that sign, they know exactly what you're talking about, and they know exactly why you're there. The gospel signs should always have both sides of the coin. The good and the bad. What I mean by this is, we're here to give the good news of Jesus Christ, but in order to do that, the bad news has to be presented as well. That's what makes the good news THE GOOD NEWS! The BAD news, choosing to be separated from God by ignoring him and the truth. To choose to be a slave to sin, to your own human desires. To die living in unrepentant sin. If you choose this way, eternal punishment and eternally being separated from God will be your final destination. The GOOD news, knowing that there is a light at the end of the tunnel, and that light is Jesus Christ. His sacrifice on the cross for our sins and him having victory over death by resurrecting three days later. We are given a chance to be set free from sin, to no longer be a slave to our sinful human desires, to no longer worry about eternal punishment, but to live with God for all eternity in heaven. It's all through Jesus Christ my friends. You might have people come up to you from time to time and tell you that what you are doing is hateful, that what you are doing is wrong. They might get offended. The thing that you have to understand here is that they're not really mad at you, they're mad at the reflection of themselves that you are showing back at them. When sins are being presented or even Jesus Christ himself, the pride of humanity takes over and they get angry and offended because you are calling them out on their own sin, on their own sinful desires, on their own lifestyle. The key here is, are they going to admit it to themselves and make a change, or keep living in unrepentant sin. For them to think that what we are doing is hateful, shows that they really don't realize what this is all about. We're here spreading the word of God because we love them, because we care about their salvation. We want them to have a chance to know God, to love God, to have fellowship with God so they can be with God in heaven for all eternity. We love them so much that we take on the mockery, the anger, and the hatred so they can have a chance to know Jesus Christ and to find peace. That's not hate my friends, that's love. They think it's hate because they're a slave to their own sins, Romans 6:16, "Know ye not, that to whom ye yield yourselves servants to obey, his servants ye are to whom ye obey; whether of sin unto death, or of obedience unto righteousness," and being a slave to their sins has put a veil over their eyes and has blinded them to a point in which they can't see the truth and can't see how devastating their actions are. Because of that, there is no accountability for their actions. They try to fill that emptiness that they have inside through any means necessary, be it by alcohol, drugs, pornography, bullying, ect..., but what they fail to recognize is that the empty space that they have inside of them can only be filled by Jesus Christ. They keep following their own human desires instead of God's. They keep following their sinful flesh, not the spirit within. We are all sinful and prideful human beings. We can't overcome sin on our own. That's why we need a Savior. That's why we need Jesus Christ. Once we are in Jesus Christ his righteousness covers us. As a Christian, the Holy Spirit holds me accountable for my actions. Before a sin can manifest in my mind and soul and take over, the Holy Spirit takes it and destroys it. For non Christians, there's no accountability. Yeah, they may feel regret, sorry, and even apologize, but they're not willing to accept and acknowledge their sin and repent for that sin. They just keep living in unrepentant sin. They just keep living a life separated from God. People might also tell you that you're judging. They'll ask, "Why are you judging?" "The bible tells you not to judge." Then they'll throw out the verse from Matthew 7:1, "Judge not, that ye be not judged." This is a prime example of someone who has just taken a verse out of context from the bible. If that person would have read the bible in context, they would have come to Matthew 7:5, "Thou hypocrite, first cast out the beam out of thine own eye; and then shalt thou see clearly to cast out the mote out of thy brother's eye." This also coincides with John 7:24, "Judge not according to the appearance, but judge righteous judgment." We are called to judge by what is right. By God's standard. We can't judge someone's actions if we are guilty of them ourselves. That's why Matthew 7:5 starts with Jesus using the word "Hypocrite." We need to dissolve our sins. We need to remove the beam from our own eye, before we can remove the mote from our brothers. If you haven't done that yet, you can't be out preaching the word of God. You would then be a part of what God hates. HYPOCRISY!

"ALWAYS SPEAK WITH COMPASSION, LOVE, AND AN OPEN HEART."

CHAPTER 8

WHAT YOU NEED TO KNOW FROM THE BIBLE BEFORE EVANGELIZING

You might be asking yourself, "How much of the bible do I need to know before I can start evangelizing?" Since evangelizing is the spreading of the gospel of Jesus Christ, all you really need to know to start out are the gospels. The four gospels, Matthew, Mark, Luke, and John. These were some of the followers of Jesus Christ filled with eyewitness accounts of Our Lord and Savior. These are four of the greatest biographies ever written about any person who has ever lived. In these gospels you learn who Jesus Christ is, his nature, his deity, his purpose on earth, his teachings, the sacrifice he made of himself for our salvation. You might also ask yourself, "Do I need to be ordained in any way in order to evangelize?" The answer is no. The great thing here is, as long as it's biblical, anyone can spread the word of God anywhere at any time, well, within the limits of the law anyways. Of course we should never end with just the gospels. All sixty-six books of the bible are the word of God. The only word of

God, and that everything should be in context. Without context, you lose the meaning of the message. Remember, context is key my friends. We should always keep learning and growing in our faith. In God's word. Never becoming stagnant. After all, God's word is our standard for everything.

"WE SHOULD ALWAYS KEEP LEARNING AND GROWING IN OUR FAITH."

CHAPTER 9

CHRISTIAN APOLOGETICS

If you want to up your knowledge game in Christianity, you should definitely check out Christian Apologetics. If you don't know what that is my friends, let me explain it to you. The word "apologetics" comes from the Greek word "apologia" which means "defense," "to have a defense for your faith." We find this usage of the word in 1st Peter 3:15, "But sanctify the Lord God in your hearts: and be ready always to give an answer to every man that asketh you a reason of the hope that is in you with meekness and fear." I believe Christian Apologetics is a must for all Christians. It's a great way to learn and grow in your faith. Christian Apologetics explains creation, our universe, our planet, and evolution with evidence and truth. It also explains the evidence for God, for Jesus Christ and the bible. Christian Apologetics gives Christians the tools to not only understand their own faith in Christianity, but to be able to explain it with evidence and truth to others. There have been many great Christian Apologists throughout the years, but in my personal opinion, the top three are Dr. Norman Geisler, Dr. Frank Turek, and Dr. William Lane Craig. Please do yourself a favor and check them out. I promise, you won't regret it.

"TRUST AND BELIEVE IN JESUS CHRIST, GOD IN HUMAN FLESH."

CHAPTER 10

THE FIRST METHOD OF EVANGELISM: PRIVATE ONE ON ONE

Congratulations my friends! Through God you are now strong, courageous, and full of wisdom to start evangelizing. The first method of evangelism that we'll talk about is perhaps the most easiest. It's called Private One on One. The reason why it's the easiest is because it consists of you only talking with people you already know like your family, friends, and coworkers. You are already in familiar territory because of you knowing them and the relationship you have with them. In my personal opinion, it's good to always have gospel tracts on hand so you have the physical word of God to give people at any time. They can take it with them and reference it whenever needed. Gospel tracts can and should be used in all three of these methods. They come in all different sizes. You can order them small enough to fit in any size wallet or purse. Of course when you engage in sharing the gospel of Jesus Christ with your family, friends, and coworkers, you might get some blow back, especially if you are a newly born again Christian. The reason for this is because they have either known you all of your life or for some time now, and they may know the sins that you have committed. The sins that you have committed by your own mouth. The sins you have committed by your own actions. It's because of this situation you might automatically be seen as a hypocrite, because they knew who you were before Christ and they might be saying to themselves, "look at this person telling me how I should live my life by the word of God. Spreading the gospel of Jesus Christ." "What right do they have to say all of this to me and be against these things when they've been guilty of it themselves?" What they don't realize is that you have been given the Holy Spirit. You've heard God's voice. You've repented of your sins and are no longer a slave to them, and you are now trying to let others know about the freedom that will come to them through Jesus Christ. Once you are given the Holy Spirit, he will show you the way, the truth, and the life through God's Son. John 14:26, "But the Comforter, which is the Holy Ghost, whom the Father will send in my name, he shall teach you all things, and bring all things to your remembrance, whatsoever I have said unto you." They too will have this epiphany if and when they finally open up their hearts and spirit to God and put their trust and belief in Jesus Christ. I believe a lot of these feelings are coming from surprise and confusion. The initial reaction might be of shock at first, but don't worry, if that happens it doesn't take long for the shock to wear off. The resistance to God is a different story. When it comes to people that you already know it hits differently because there's a connection and intimacy that's different with them than with someone down the street that you don't know, but

God says to love your neighbor as yourself, Leviticus 19:18, "Thou shalt not avenge, nor bear any grudge against the children of thy people, but thou shalt love thy neighbour as thyself: I am the Lord." God is of love, God is love, and he tells us all to love everyone, 1st John 4:7-8, "Beloved, let us love one another, for love is of God; and every one that loveth is born of God, and knoweth God. He that loveth not knoweth not God; for God is love." Love is giving people the truth, even if they don't want to hear it. To see family members, friends, and strangers heading down a path of spiritual suicide aches my heart, and we as Christians should take ever opportunity that we have to try to redirect them to safety, redirect them to the truth, redirect them to God. When it comes to talking to people you know about Jesus Christ, if they are closed off, not spiritual open, or just don't want to talk about it, these moments are best done in small increments. If you push the subject too hard to someone who doesn't want the conversation, you're risking the possibility of that relationship being cut off completely, and never getting the opportunity again to share the word of God with them. There's only so much you can do. If they're too closed off and shut down to the truth, the only thing you can do is let them know that you're there for them whenever they're ready to talk or if they have any questions. For the ones who are receptive to conversations about God, This is the time to open up the floodgates and by using compassion, love, and encouragement let them know about The Son of God, Our Lord Jesus Christ.

> "HE THAT LOVETH NOT KNOWETH NOT GOD; FOR GOD IS LOVE." 1ST JOHN 4:8

CHAPTER 11

THE SECOND METHOD OF EVANGELISM: PUBLIC ONE ON ONE

The next method of evangelism that we're going to talk about is Public One on One. This takes you from the comforts of familiarity to a public setting. People you don't know. People you have never met before. The thought of this can be scary and anxiety filled, but this method can ease this anxiety by the fact that you're just handing out gospel tracts to people one on one without saying a single word. Just handing them a tract and moving on. Now if someone actually wants to talk to you after you give them the tract, then you can use the wisdom and skill that you've already used with your family and friends to elaborate more or to answer any questions they may have, but it'll be a one on one situation. You and them. In my experience this is extraordinarily rare. Most people take it either knowing what it is or not knowing at all, or they just wave you off. What they don't realize is, at that moment you've just given them the way to eternal life. They just have to open up their heart and spirit and acknowledge it. This method is a wonderful way to get the gospel of Jesus Christ out to the people in public without actually having to open-air preach. This method also builds up your confidence as you navigate through the public space armed with the word of God. When you're out there, you'll notice that not only are you getting more confident, but the foundation of your faith is getting stronger, and you'll start to feel any anxiety that you once had start to dissipate. The more often you do this, the more you start feeling relaxed and calm. Unfortunately I see many Christians that are afraid to express their faith. Afraid to be THAT person who goes around and talks about Jesus Christ all the time. They're afraid of what people might think. Of what the world might think. Let me tell you something my friends, we should never care about what the world thinks of us. The only thing that matters is what God thinks of us. The world will persecute us. The world will be angry with us. The world will do whatever it can to fight that burning truth that lies within. The world can lie to itself all it wants, but it can never lie to God. No matter what kind of hatred is projected on us, never forget what Jesus Christ said in John 15:18, "If the world hate you, ye know that it hated me before it hated you." We are not alone, my friends. What we go through as disciples, as followers of Christ is what Jesus Christ, his apostles, and his disciples throughout the years have gone through long before you and I came along. They died for their faith. They died trying to save people. They died for telling people how they could live forever in heaven with God. My friends, just like Noah, he was delivered from the sin of the world by ignoring the destruction around him and focused just on God's instructions. The instructions that would save him. The building of the Ark. Jesus Christ is our Ark. We just need to follow him. With him we are delivered from sin and destruction. With him we are no longer slaves to sin.

"THE WORLD CAN LIE TO ITSELF ALL IT WANTS, BUT IT CAN NEVER LIE TO GOD."

CHAPTER 12

THE THIRD METHOD OF EVANGELISM: OPEN-AIR PREACHING

Welcome friends to the last and final method of evangelism. This one is something else. This one will challenge all of your senses. It will put all of your knowledge, wisdom, courage, and strength to the test, but with God on your side, he will guide you through it all. What we're talking about here is Open-air Preaching. This is when you are in public, either amplified or not with gospel tracts in hand, preaching the gospel of Jesus Christ to every person around. This is the most difficult method of evangelism because you are literally on the front lines preaching the word of God. You will realize quickly that having tough skin is a necessity in this method of evangelism. That is why we Christians are all given the armor of God. Ephesians 6:11, "Put on the whole armour of God, that ye may be able to stand against the wiles of the devil." God said in 1st John 3:8, "He that committeth sin is of the devil." What that means is whoever keeps living in unrepentant sin is of the devil. The ones who keep sinning and don't do anything about it. The devil and his demons try to do three things to us. They try to deceive us. They try to tempt us. Then they try to destroy us. The devil wants to do everything he can to turn as many people away from God as possible. You will face many who are like this on the streets. The ones who are of the devil. In Fact the majority of the world lives like this. They live subjectively. They don't care about facts. They don't care about evidence. All they care about is their own personal feelings. What makes them feel good. What makes them happy. They live by their own human sinful flesh. They become slaves to it. They become slaves to their human desires. All logic is thrown out the window my friends. Galatians 6:7-8, "Be not deceived; God is not mocked: for whatsoever a man soweth, that shall he also reap. For he that soweth to his flesh shall of the flesh reap corruption; but he that soweth to the Spirit shall of the Spirit reap life everlasting." This sinful, prideful lifestyle will only bring corruption and destruction to yourself and those around you. Just ask anyone who is living a life of addiction, living a life of being a slave to themselves. On the other hand, living for the spirit, will bring everlasting life and peace. It will open the door to God. That's why evangelism needs to be done my friends. Without someone spreading God's word, how is it going to reach the eyes and ears of the lost. We bring the truth and evidence into their life. We bring the word of God into their life. We bring to them the only way for salvation, JESUS CHRIST! Remember, Jesus Christ said, "I am THE way." He did not say, "I am A way." He is the only way to heaven my friends.

"PUT ON THE WHOLE ARMOUR OF GOD, THAT YE MAY BE ABLE TO STAND AGAINST THE WILES OF THE DEVIL."
EPHESIANS 6:11

CHAPTER 13

CALL ONTO GOD AND HE WILL ANSWER

The evangelism methods that are in this book are arranged in this particular order to help you get over any fear or self doubt that you may have so you can slowly and confidently go from one method to the next from Private One on One to Public One on One to finally Open-air Preaching with ease. Each method gives you the tools to move on to the next, and before you know it, you'll be glorifying God's name in front of crowds of people. We all have the capability of doing this. It's all up to you on how far you want to go. It's all up to you my friends. I've said it before, our purpose in life is to glorify God and to have fellowship with him. To have a loving and intimate relationship with him. Taking time everyday to just pray to God. To talk to God. To talk about things that are on your mind, in your life, and asking him for the strength and wisdom to get through any hardship that you might be dealing with. He's always listening my friends. Jeremiah 33:3, "Call unto thee, and I will answer thee, and show thee great and mighty things, which thou knowest not." You are wonderfully and beautifully made and we all have self-worth because we are all made in God's image. It's fitting that the last command Jesus Christ gave us Christians was to share and teach his word, to share and teach the gospel to all creation so that every single person on earth can have the chance to know the truth, to know true love, to know peace, to know GOD! Thank you so much for taking the time to read this book. I'm so thankful and blessed that God has given me the wisdom and strength to have created something that can encourage other Christians to answer this command of Jesus Christ. The call to evangelize. I hope this book was insightful, informational, and has given you a better understanding of what evangelism really is, and why we need it so badly. The tools and information that I have given you in this book will help you as you navigate down this road of evangelism. God will be there with you every step of the way, guiding you. Like Isaiah 58:11 says, "And the Lord shall guide thee continually." No one will pluck you out of his hand, John 10:28. God's embrace will always keep you safe and protected. My thoughts and prayers are with you as you make this journey. With tremendous love and gratitude, I thank you, and may God bless you all!

"I AM ALPHA AND OMEGA, THE BEGINNING AND THE END, THE FIRST AND THE LAST." REVELATION 22:13

About the Author

Matt Hertzberg is an Evangelist, a Christian Apologist, and the founder of the YouTube channel "Spreading the Seed of Truth." Besides traveling around preaching and teaching the word of God, he also enjoys spending time with family and friends. Matt resides in the beautiful state of Wisconsin with his wife and their dog Chloe.

Milton Keynes UK
Ingram Content Group UK Ltd.
UKHW021354011224
451693UK00012B/837